SONG OF A FATHERLESS CHILD

a collection of poetry by
Ginny Knight

photographs and afterword by Leon Knight

TA Publications
P.O. Box 22583
Minneapolis, MN 55422

International Standard Book Number 0-9635690-6-6
Library Of Congress Catalog Card Number 94-61862
Copyright © 1994 TA Publications

ALL RIGHTS RESERVED
Reproduction in whole or in part without written permission is prohibited,
except by a reviewer who may quote brief passages in a review.

Printed in the United States of America

CONTENTS

I Wanted Family .... Dedication
for Leon

What We Are 1
Pecan Tree (2) 1
Grandmother 2
Mother 3
Silence 3
Daddy 4
Song Of A Fatherless Child 4
What My Cup Can Hold 5
Orphans 5
Patchwork Quilt 6
Journey To Phoenix 7
Aunt Ollie 8
Home Baked Bread 8
Inheritance — History 9
My Genealogy 9
Triumphant Time 10
For Aunt Ollie 10
Bend In The Trail 11
Lucy's Little Girl 11
Double-Dutch 12
I Want To Think Of Summer 12
The Fool 13
Cosmos 13
Family Heirloom 14
Time In The Old Neighborhood .. 14
Anna Of The Back Steps 15
Myths 15
Roots 16
Patterns Rewoven 16
Circles In The Sand 17
Earth Visit 17
Edge Of The Earth 18
Of Snow And Sand 19
Isn't This My Place? 19
Waiting For Rain 20
Secrets 20
Days 21
Inside Out 21
I Am The One In Need 22
Crippled 22
Walking On The Lake 23
Hour Glass 23
Scars 24
Illness 24

I Am Becoming Selfish 25
Always Here 25
Day Breaks 26
Quiet Desert Sounds 26
Storm 27
Not The Same 27
Vacation 28
Spring Begins In Inverness 28
The Earth 29
Fog Wrapped Day 29
March 1986 30
Chameleon Sort Of Day 30
Foreshortened Summer 31
River Road In Autumn 31
Ritual Celebration 32
Tracery Of Winter 32
A Gift 33
Except For You 33
Thoughts Of You 34
Length Of Days 34
If I Were A Poet 35
I Remember 35
I Want To Grow Old 36
Accidental Dance 36
Family Tree 37
Tapestry 37
Destiny 38
Theresa And I 38
Through The Looking Glass 39
City Nights In Winter 40
Primeval Heart 40
Our Children 41
Something Lost 41
Rage Of Poetry 42
Now That It Is Winter 42
Soldier Boys 43
Sing Me No Warrior Songs 43
1989 44
Will We Never Learn 44
Can It Be A Love Song 45
A Bright Red Tulip 45
Naming Reality 46
Fall 1992 46
The Stone Of Rememberance 47
It Shouldn't Have Been Like That 47
Where Children Play 48
Blood Brothers 48

Same Ol' Snake 49	They Tap At My Window 60
Dèjá Vu 49	Chinese Sister 60
No More New Land 50	Forever On The Wing 61
The Garden 50	In The Stillness 61
Land Of My Youth 51	The Poet 62
Why Are We Here? 51	Red Brick House 62
Once I Flew 52	Born Of Earth And Sun 63
Not A Pearl 52	The Nature Of My Soul 63
Memories Go 53	Walking In Obscurity 64
I Am There (Zimbabwe) 53	The Skipping Stone 64
A Time When Zimbabwe 54	Barefoot In Summer 65
Apartheid 54	Summer Solstice 65
Elder Sister 55	Through Yun's Eyes 66
Soweto School Girl 55	I Like To Feel You Near 66
The Acacia Tree 56	Unfocused 67
Sometimes I Dream You 56	Good Things 67
Bonds Of Family 57	Nightmare 68
African River 57	Canyon Walk 68
Daughters Of Eve 58	My Treasure 69
We Are All God's Children 58	Call Of The Canyon 69
Storm Warning 59	
View Out Of Africa 59	Afterword by Leon Knight 70

for Leon
I WANTED FAMILY

I wanted family
    some connection
    proof I am
        alive

you wrote me on a page
    books filled of us
I stitched you in thread
    a tapestry

not some taped together
    chapbook
or clumsy knitted thing
but art framed and bound
    lining walls
    filling shelves

we two
are a family
    you and me

Weaver bird tree — Sibanda's farm, Botswana

WHAT WE ARE

memory goes its way
bringing images to life
    regardless of desire
like Spring
has somewhere gone
and comes again
    a blossoming day

memory in shadow hides
pushing through accumulated mulch
to reveal bright moments
    sharp as crocus leaves
not forgotten
    merely kept aside

memory descends in streams
moving ripples repeating patterns
held in history
    stored in dreams

when time falls apart
memory is after all
    what we are

PECAN TREE (2)

Time stood still
    summers
when I climbed
    the pecan tree
a rough branch
    curved
    to hold me safe
    above earthly worries
fuzzy catkins danced
    at the slightest breeze
and feathery leaves parted
to reveal a sky
    bluer than the one I saw
    from the ground
I lay on the rough bark
    and listened to
    my heart

GRANDMOTHER

Grandmother,
      I never even heard of you
      till I was grown.
Now I look for you everywhere.
Those high cheekbones
      in my mirror:
      are they yours?
Or my small feet?

From what I know of grandfather
you might be Shawnee
      or Dakota
      or even Cherokee.
I wear soft moccasins,
      placing my feet
      in every print I see.
            But they don't fit.

      * * * * *

      I am a stranger.
      I have no history.

      * * * * *

As a girl,
      did you live in a tipi?
      or sing of Custer's fall?
      did you learn to soften deerskin?
      or know the eagle's call?

      * * * * *

you must have missed me sometimes,
tears behind your eyelids tight,
and empty arms folded,
      waiting for me
           and a kiss goodnight.

But I can never find you:
my own eyes mist with tears
      my feet stumble
      my arms ache
as I wander empty years.

           still a stranger
           still without a past
           still wearing moccasins
                following
                fading prairie paths.

MOTHER

You kept your secrets
    very well
you hid them away from me
    your first-born child
so that I do not know
    you
    or my genealogy

Now that you are gone
I carry your secrets
    out of their dark
    hiding places
exposed to the light
    they crumble in my hands
    the bits and pieces
    spreading like a stain
    down the front of my dress
the way the cover
on the bible
    of your father
        (my grandfather —
        though I do not know his name)
broke and crumbled
when I tried to turn a page

SILENCE

silence is strong
    tearing at the bond
        between us
rending apart the seams
    we've sewn

stillness is kind
    helping the need
    to contemplate
solitude is mulch
    to help
    love grow

but silence is sharp
    cutting the ties
    that once held
        us close

DADDY

Daddy came home
      once
that I remember

his presence filled the tiny house —
the screaming and fighting
shook the walls
      like a wind storm

we watched with sideways glances
afraid to look at him directly

when he left it was as if
we had been holding
      our breath
and life went back to normal

years later I was called
to his bedside   as he lay
      dying

I couldn't comprehend
      that small shrunken figure

from that visit
so many years before —
his visit that had
so overwhelmed us
      those few days
I had thought he was
      a big man

SONG OF A FATHERLESS CHILD

father
      you are like the slave owner
          of old
      sowing your seed in shame
          hiding your lineage
          from your children
you left
      without seeing our faces
      knowing nothing of our promise
      gaining no reward as parent
      sharing no joy that we attain

we would have sung
      your praises
but we do not know your name

WHAT MY CUP CAN HOLD
for father (unknown)

I had wanted you to say
    I love you
it should have been
easy to write "love"
though pencil and paper
    are soulless
    chips of wood
but a daughter should hear
    I love you
a cupful each morning
    good for growing
    like calcium for bones
I wanted no more
    than my cup
    could hold

ORPHANS
for my brother

Silence has broken
the connection
    (it was tenuous anyway)

For years I struggled
to make sense of it
    while you
    screamed
    your rage

We are orphans now
    (I have been
    for a long time)
the severed cord
dangles
in silence

PATCHWORK QUILT

I am not of a piece.
    I was shaped
and stitched together   by women,
each with her own pattern,
a vision   committed to memory.

Great Aunt Ollie.
    She could do anything.
    "If it's worth doing,
    it's worth doing well," she'd say.

    Flowers bloomed in her footprints.

    The house, scrubbed
        and polished,
    smelled of fresh-baked bread.

    She sewed me
    in straight, determined stitches —
    "If you really want to,   you can do it."

    She placed moccasins   on my feet
    and a precious silver-bird   in my hand.

Helen, Mother,
    took up the stitching
    with trembling hands.

    Child-like   uneven stitches,
    hoping to make lace —
    but knots   got in her way.

    The books she gave me
        led me
    where she was afraid to go.

Mrs. Smith,
    surrogate for the grandmother
    I never knew.

    Arthritic hands
    carefully, painfully   creating a pattern
    my childish fingers could follow
    when   (bent and misshapen)
        hers could not.

    "Do the things that must be done,
    but don't forget to sing the stars
    and dance around the sun."

She sparkled my eyes
with moondust
and gave me a sewing kit
I carry with me   everywhere.

I am not of a piece.
My stitches   do not match.
I push the stuffing back inside
and carefully trim the edges
          where I'm frayed.

My own stitching
drawing the pieces   together
where others left off.
Making my own   pattern
          with the stitching
          I have learned.

JOURNEY TO PHOENIX —
a memorial for mother

It is appropriate
that the plane is engulfed
in clouds
          as I think of you
outside the window
they float by
          soft and fluffy
but causing jolts and bumps
as we pass through

you remind me
of those clouds

From a distance
          I could see you clearly
but when I got close
          you dissipated
                    into fog
I wanted to reach out to you
          but how do I
          capture a cloud?

So I sit in the airplane
watch the clouds
and think
          of you

AUNT OLLIE

Winter nights
>she held me on her lap
>plump arms protecting
>>tight around me
>>the monotonous creaking of the chair
>>>shielding me from violence

Summer nights
>we walked long dark streets
>she held my hand tightly
>the monotonous sound of our footsteps
>erasing from my mind
>>sounds of violence

She is gone —
>I am no more that skinny trembling child
>>my life is peaceful
>no need now for monotony

But sometimes
>the echo of hate heard in a distant
>>slamming door
>makes my heart jump my legs shake

then I long for the sound
>of her voice telling stories
>of the happy scenes we saw
>walking past brightly lit
>>houses
>>>quiet
>>in the summer
>>>night.

HOME BAKED BREAD

Once a week she baked bread
mixing flour and yeast and
>kneading....
tenderly blanketing the loaves in a warm place
she went about
>sweeping.... dusting....
>>kneading....
In dough rising she missed good times
>sometimes....
the crusty brown loaves
were taken for granted by others....
>not by her
sweaty and uncomfortable
in the too-warm kitchen
>kneading.... kneading....
>>needing....

INHERITANCE — HISTORY
(from Mother)

like a puzzle
the bits and pieces
    of your life
lie scattered before me

you left no instructions
and I am not clever enough
to fit them together
    on my own

finally my fingers
are sore and raw
from sifting
    and turning

I will pack what remains
    in a box
to store away
in my closet

the connection is finally broken
    I will not forget you
even though I do not
    understand

MY GENEALOGY

This history was learned
    too late
    to be real
It needed
    a creaking rocking chair
    and warm encircling arms
    in the telling

Faded photographs
    presented to my
    age-dimmed eyes
    reveal only shadows
Fathers and grandfathers
    are only dates
    on cold tombstones
    marking my genealogy

TRIUMPHANT TIME

time betrays
past   invading present
reviving feelings I thought
     long buried

overlapping time disorients me
     like double-vision
I am heavy with remembrance

confusing child and adult
history burns my soul
     time triumphs

FOR AUNT OLLIE
who mothered me for almost eleven years

I was angry
    felt deserted
         when you died
it was so lonely — left on my own
     I was only eleven

"You will forget me" you said
"never visit my grave"

I never did return to that
     unfamiliar place
I don't think of you there
but you were wrong
     I will never forget you

sometimes I can't remember
the way you looked
     (photographs are no help)
but then I hear the words
     you used to say
     coming from my lips

wisdom spoken
     from generation
     to generation

BEND IN THE TRAIL
for my mother Helen Roberts Grant, 1905-1984

I can't see
beyond the bend
      in the path
but I know it curves
into the woods
and climbs the hill

The trail of dark damp earth
marked with the iridescent
leaves of fall
      is more enticing to me
      than Dorothy's
      yellow brick road

Curiosity pulls me
I want to know the secrets
hidden in the sumac
      glowing red
just around the bend
in the trail

LUCY'S LITTLE GIRL

grown now
      looking for secrets
      no longer afraid
she called
      long distance

her voice clear
      as if the secrets
            were not threatening
      as if the past
            was not terrible

she said,
      "This is Donna
      Lucy's girl"

DOUBLE-DUTCH

I remember
>> warm crayola-colored days
>> where slapping ropes
>> beat our rhyme in dust-time

> *one-two-three-four*
>> *Mama's standin'*
>> *at the door*
> *five-six-seven-eight*
>> *shes gonna getcha*
>> *if you're late*

I remember
>> the summer sun   my pounding heart
>> pumping the rhythm of the ropes
>> and chanting friends urging me on
>>> playing games helped ease the pain

I remember double-dutch

I WANT TO THINK OF SUMMER

I want to think of summer

of pomegranates
>> hanging, plump and ripe
>> over the back fence
how we sat in the dusty shade
> of eucalyptus
peeling open the tough leathery-skin
> to reveal
the glistening jewel-like
> seed within
how the blood-red juice would stain
> our lips and fingers
and trickle thankful down
our dry, parched throats

Bitter times are best forgot
but   sometimes
I want to think of summer
> and pomegranates

THE FOOL

You think I am a clown
covered as I am with patches

But I have learned
      hurt feeds
          upon itself
              growing wild
                  festering,
              squeezing,
          choking,
      polluting the soul

So I cover each pain
with a bright new patch
    and
        play
            the
                fool

COSMOS

My ineffectual scratching in the soil
has produced a few
        scraggly cosmos
flowers faded pale
in the too-bright
too-hot sun
        I wonder "What does it take
        to make something grow?"
My energy is drained
by unrelenting heat
I sit in a narrow
      spot of shade
my back against the rough
still-warm stucco
      of the wall
my hair hangs
      hot and heavy on my back

I empty a small bucket of water
      over the flowers
and watch it disappear
into the thirsty soil
and will the cosmos
      "grow"

FAMILY HEIRLOOM

From a distance
the colors blend into
a pleasing pattern
    but the threads have become
    unimaginatively tangled

Woven in disregard
stretched and pulled
without design
    the skein distorted
    from its purpose

It will take a lifetime
for the most dexterous hands
    to unravel these knots

TIME IN THE OLD NEIGHBORHOOD

women defined
the old neighborhood
    there were men
        but mostly
        they were shadowy
        background figures

the voices
behind screen doors
    chiding   entreating
    warning   calling
were women's voices

women set
    chore-time   play-time
    lunch-time
we thought we were
    free
but we followed time
    set by the women
    of the neighborhood

ANNA OF THE BACK STEPS

    her name was Anna
    but   in the way of children
                we called her
                        Annie
    she acknowledged Annie
    but kept herself apart
            knowing she was different

    Anna had more chores
    than any of the rest of us
            she did all the housework
                  and cooking
    she ate bread fried in lard
            for breakfast
    her clothes never fit her well

    the neighbors said Anna's mother
            was worldly
    she wore big fancy hats
    played the piano
        in a bar
                at night
    Anna said her mother had read
            Anna Karenina

    in late afternoon
            after the shade reached
            the back of her house
    Anna sat on the back steps
            listening
    as her mother practiced
            the piano

MYTHS

    we build our own myths
    to change the contours
        of our lives

    the contradiction between
            thought and reality
    can become a chasm
            making an interesting
                climb up
            or an impossible trap

ROOTS

My roots
are in the desert
      buried deep
      in warm coarse sand.

I feel fragile in the snow
like a foreigner
      I do not understand
      the sounds
the language
      falls in soft flakes
      around my ears
piling up
      making the path slippery
      under my feet

PATTERNS REWOVEN

this weaving is a constant thing
threads of contradiction
      pulling at fragile fabric
reflections changing
      hue and intensity
      at the unexpected splintering
      of a day

resistance doesn't click
      with truth
holes torn of mourning
      constantly
      need mending
while shadows dance
      with mottled grace
behind the wispy veil of memory

in stitching up the past
the fabric is made stronger
      the pattern
      made more vivid
a never ending restoration

patterns of our lives
      rewoven
      day by day

CIRCLES IN THE SAND

we walk the earth
    we have
      a place here
our shadows are dreams
      merged to history
our footprints mark songs
      wind-tossed in the air
    we breath

uneasy we walk the ridge
bemused by shadows
      our steps form
      circles in the sand

EARTH VISIT

like drops of rain
we visit earth
      making little difference
      alone
yet coming together
we make a pond
      or river flowing

the earth longs
for a stream
      and fruiting
thirsts for renewing
      generations

yet one rain drop
      evaporating
does not end the tide
      no difference
      is noted
as one visit ends

EDGE OF THE EARTH

Over sage and sand,
surrounded by grey-blue
mountains that float
on morning mist,
        we climb
        through tamarisk
        and cedar.

At each turn the sun
lights new colors
on the hills,
        blinding our eyes
        to man-made dangers.

We walk through fouled air
        clicking rocks
and   water not safe
            for drinking.

Through aspen's trembling leaves
into dark shadows
        of ponderosa.

With pine-soft steps,
we climb
        until
many-colored rocks
lead us
        through piñon
up to   the edge
        of the earth.

From here we can see
        forever,
danger forgotten far below,
and we are intoxicated
        with the sweet smell
        and strange beauty
        of cliff rose.

OF SNOW AND SAND

The wind swept patterns
in the snow
reminding me of warmer
      more congenial places
chunks of snow
piled in reckless abandon
like boulders
      in Papago Park

An anemic desert
      bled of color
         unwarmed by winter's sun
yet crystals sparkle
      in the snow
like mica in the sand

ISN'T THIS MY PLACE?

Warm sand harsh beneath my feet.
A cloak of sunshine warms my arms.
Dry wind caresses my skin.

A trickle of water sounds
      so far away.
Green grass shimmers,
      a mirage.
Berries hang heavy
on dimly seen boughs.

This cold in my bones
      is not real
a magician's trick.
Icy landscapes,
      a dream.

Reality is hard rough stones.
Cool shadows, burning
      sunshine.
Dust rising in swirls
      after my feet.
No footprints left to show
I've been here.

WAITING FOR RAIN

in drought
everything waits . . .
        promise held
. . . waits for rain

a light breeze
        raises hope
        and dust
far away lightning
        cracks the evening

if it comes
        the life renewing rain
drought will disappear
        in blossoming and green
and hope
        washed and restored
        will revive the cycle

early this electric morning
promising large drops
        pocked the earth
dark clouds
        churned and rolled
        across the sky
only to be pulled away
        impotent
as lightning boomed
        far away
and hope
        was choked
        by swirling dust
        devils

SECRETS

the earth keeps answers
we don't know
how to question
        woodland secrets
            held in Yew
        ocean wisdom
            beyond imagination
it is not yet time
to venerate the stars

DAYS

There are days
    the sun does not
    warm or brown
    my skin
the breeze
    does not lift my hair
    or cool my brow
when there is no echo
    marking my footsteps
    in the hall
and when I look around
    I see I have
    no shadow
        at all.

INSIDE OUT

fever turns me
        inside out
raw seams showing
thread-ends dangling

in dark hours
    discomfort
unravels memories
    that itch my skin
    like cockroaches
        crawling
my careful patching
    comes undone

a melting chill drips
    cooling me
turning fever
        upside down
but I am left
feeling ragged
    uneasy with
    remembering
and still turned
    inside out

I AM THE ONE IN NEED

behind the rough wall
I scratch the earth
    around the cutting
    I have planted
        a gift from my mother
my nails split
and the dark rings
under my eyes
    fill
    spilling drops upon
    my plant

the plant is tough
its roots deep
    it grows
    leaning
        against the wall
when I walk near
its thorns
scratch my legs
    causing blood to flow
    upon
    my plant

look at me bleed
I am the one in need

CRIPPLED

the past clings
    an irritant
    like sand in my shoe
i cannot shake off
    this history

i limp along
leaning on your strength
the blister on my heel
    bandaged
    to ward off
        infection

WALKING ON THE LAKE

I could walk on the lake
    filled with clouds
    and smooth as glass
        pretending shallow
        hiding deep
it is true
the sky has fallen
turned the lake upside down
spilling not a drop
nor revealing
    twisting slimy things
    that float in muck
    underneath illusion

HOUR GLASS

Time sifts slowly
in measured grains
    silently
creating a new form
for which I am
    totally unprepared

I am surprised to find at the core
    a resilience —
    a strength unseen —
pulling together parts
that otherwise might crack
    or break
in resistance
to this terrible thing

Like the walls of the canyon
    sand cemented to strength
    holding suspended
        fossils
history of time in time
    unprepared
now resistant to unknown
    terrors
        in new forms

My time sifts
    in measured grains
        slowly

SCARS

I have peeled away
the ugly scars
expecting the flesh
    underneath
to be raw and painful
    but it is not

my skin is leather now
    tough
future wounds will not go
    so deep
and you will have to look
    very close
to see the tiny welts
of past hurt that remain

ILLNESS

Illness brought a
    cold, glaring
        awful reality
that almost killed my dreams

but there is something in me
that couldn't let them go

so I pruned them back
and nurtured them
    in my secret place

my dreams grow smaller now
for illness chases foolish fantasies

all that is left of dreams
    once lush and full
are roots
    too deep
    to notice drought
and tiny leaves folded tight
    around the stunted branches
        that remain

I AM BECOMING SELFISH

I am becoming selfish
unwilling to fit my life
to someone else's scheme
the time left is too short
to spend
on someone else's dream

the world will not stop
or even sigh
when I am gone
      so
I am becoming selfish

only I can sing my song
and it really doesn't matter
that no one sings along

ALWAYS HERE

I am always here
stretched over time
like the light of stars
      long dead

my ashes sift into sand
helping desert flowers
      grow

I am part of the universe
flowing over earth
like fog or rain
      feeding rivers

my bones turn to mulch
helping wild flowers
      bloom

I am always here
      part of the universe
      stretched over time

DAY BREAKS

This day breaks
with rude city sounds
      mechanical rumblings
      shattering the night
      tormenting dreams
      with brazen light

But I know somewhere
      dawn comes
with soft bird sounds
      carefully folding dreams
      into soft shadows
safely held for some future
      sleepless night

QUIET DESERT SOUNDS

I had forgotten
quiet desert sounds
flickering across unending azure sky
    not the secretive
      quiet of northern woods
        but
sounds of mourning doves
and crunching sand
as we walk in dappled shade
under spreading desert trees

ancient quiet
held in walls
      Hohokam* walls
      of caliche**
inhabited now by lizards
and chirping birds

*Those who have gone
**Pronounced Cuh-lee-chee

STORM

Thunder cracked the day
      heavy with foreboding
rain slashed the sudden dark
      with sharp impatience
angry clouds spewed
      fierce, threatening,
      ominous, warnings
          for me

I long for fresh washed quiet
      blue sky mirrored
      in glassy pools
remnants of a storm
I must endure

NOT THE SAME

from the cliff
we could not hear
      the ocean
as it spread
lacy fans of foam
on the beach
      below
then in silent retreat
washed rocks
      glistening black

from the cliff
we could not feel
      the sand
or smell ocean salt
even the damp mist
did not rise to moist
      our skin

the view from the heights
is beautiful
      but not the same

VACATION

We started on
       a fog-soft morning.
Along the way
sun flowers   stood
      heads bowed
           waiting...

Busy morning sounds
reached our ears
    mist-muted

We saw small birds
      lined up on wires,
      feathers fluffed
         watching
the water-colored landscape.

Later, on a fence post,
a meadowlark sang
    the arrival
        of the sun.

SPRING BEGINS IN INVERNESS
(20 March, 1982)

The rising fog
    unveils rounded hills
    across Tamale Bay
the sun
    released from clouds
    trickles down
    through fragrant eucalyptus stands
      to silver grass
      and warm the sand
      where marsh mice play
the breeze awakens
    moss hung trees
    and gently carries
    soaring birds
      over water
      where now
        the sun dances
        joyously
        on the tops of waves

THE EARTH

The earth
    does not regret
        or hate
    accepting
        all blood and bones
        without tears
    judging not
        the reason
        for interment
    using all
        to regenerate

FOG-WRAPPED DAY

fog envelopes lake and woods
making sky and earth its own
    muting sounds
    stopping time

a wet, heavy fog
    not melancholy
but hiding contradictions

on the sandy beach
    where gulls huddle
laughing waves chase each other
rushing in to tickle the shore
    with frothy fingers

the volcanic strand further on
    is washed
obsidian black, glistening
from lake's more insistent waves

through the fog
waves' healing rhythms
splash against the rocks
    below our room,
wash away anxiety

a sassy gull
    made brave by fog
struts by our window
ignoring the moist beauty
of the fog-wrapped lake
    cocking its head
    looking for crumbs

MARCH 1986

The greening begins at the edge
of the damp dark woods
where the stream has broken free of ice
and rushes joyfully to the meadow

From beneath the mat
of last year's leaves
tender buds push upwards
sprouting a promise of spring

Full thirty years we've shared
       and watched as many springs
each new blossoming a marvel
to treasure and record

Each spring now a victory

CHAMELEON SORT OF DAY

the green edge of summer
       moss soft and ripe
brushes the chameleon
       days of autumn

sun colors caught up in leaves
spill dappled across our path
to nestle — red and gold
         in grass

beneath ripening grain
the still-green of summer
teases us with breezes
that rattle sun-burnt
       colored leaves
       and fill the wood
       with autumn sounds

meanwhile ducks and geese
       flock south
not fooled as we
by this   chameleon
         sort of day

FORESHORTENED SUMMER

fidgety and ill tempered
the wind
scraped humid air
        into angry gray clouds

frantic bursts of lightning
slashed heavy skies
spilling ever more water into
        swollen rivers

in the flooded heartland
we are no match
        for nature
the drought is ended
summer is washed away

RIVER ROAD IN AUTUMN

the fiery glow of sumac
        lights the river way
across straw-colored fields
        of ripe grain
autumn covered hills rise
        to reflect in pools
        left of summer's flood

the river flows already winter-dark
rushing to sea before the coming freeze

in a dead or dying stand
one tree seems alive
        branches covered with
        the green of spring
it is illusion though
a vine's embrace hides
        dead limbs
seeks to trick us with leaves
        while tendrils choke
        sap's flow

the river hurries uncaring by
holding terrible secrets in its depths

we turn from the swamp where trees die
to enjoy autumn's colorful show
we do not want to think of what
        the river carries
        in the undertow

RITUAL CELEBRATION

we celebrate with small rituals
    coffee shared
    and conversation
warm behind steamed
    streaming windows
while cold bright sun
lights icy spikes
    of grass
        sparkling
    above the frozen
    crust of snow

TRACERY OF WINTER

The early snow
    moist and clinging
covers the tangle of woods
    damp and dark
        in outline
    like a scratchboard drawing
the beauty of it
    hides the icy
    treacherous places
covers the confusion
    of branches
    dry grass
    and dead leaves
pristine
    it sparkles
    under the weak
    winter sun
revealing
    an intricate
    tracery
    of winter

A GIFT

I like the flow of days
        unnumbered
into years
        uncounted
with the natural rhythm
        of tide
        and seasons
we don't need to count
        years and days
we need only to
        remember the rhythms
        the good seasons
                warm and wonderful
        a gift
                unnamed

EXCEPT FOR YOU

I am solitary
        taciturn to many
        not with you

                outside the wind is raw
                hurls leaves against
                        my window
                whips through trees
                      like an angry oracle
                      thinking it can
                      determine my fate
                it scatters twigs and leaves
                across my path
                bends trees
                      almost to breaking
                      limbs scraping helplessly
                      against my walls

                inside with you
                I am warm
                      the sound of the storm
                      seems far away

Except for you
I would be lost
        in the storm

THOUGHTS OF YOU

My mind is filled
with thoughts
    of you.
I hold them
    carefully
like lantern slides.

As my eyes adjust
    to memories
bright images fill
    my heart.

There is the moon
shining like
    a lantern
showing us secret places
    beneath the waves.

On the warm
    moist sand
    of the beach
our footprints
dance in patterns
    of delight.

LENGTH OF DAYS

spring has not yet come
    to this place
though there is promise
in the length of days

it was spring
    by the ocean
those many years ago
our garden bloomed
    and oh,
the things we did not know

but love has grown
and blossomed
    and spring —
    spring still holds promise
in the length of days

IF I WERE A POET

If I were a poet
I would
       gather words
       to delight you,
beautiful words
       sounding
       my love
clear and sweet
       like a silver
       flute

I REMEMBER
for Leon

I have no need for dreams
of mystical or magical places
or fantasies of wealth or fame

for I remember
       a grassy hill
       in California
       you brought me
       wildflowers

       a foggy day
       in London
       where we walked
             hand in hand
       and shared our lunch
       in Russell Square

       warm days
       we spent
       under fragrant African trees
             we found
       a daughter's love

       the hard times
       made easier to bear
       by the love
             we share

       and I still
       smell the scent
       of wildflowers

I WANT TO GROW OLD

I want to grow old
      in my time
see lines mark my face

I don't want to hide
my sagging elbows
under "graceful" sleeves
or "wash away the gray"

I want to grow old
to share the years with you
see age upon your face
and watch grandchildren
      grow

ACCIDENTAL DANCE

we joined this
      dance
not knowing the rhythms
      and patterns
that lay ahead

the surprise is
      how in tune
      we are
and how the choreography
      unplanned
is graceful and beautiful

perhaps too much planning
      and rehearsing
would have taken away
      some of the joy
we have found in this quite
      accidental
      dance

FAMILY TREE

the seed was planted
    haphazardly
blown into a crevice
    by the wind of chance
a survivor
    it sprouted
    tough and flexible
pushing aside the concrete
    that threatened
        to entomb it
it will never grow
    straight and tall
but there is beauty
    in its twisted shape
    and comfort in its shade

TAPESTRY

My days and years
are woven together
in an intricate tapestry
    banded by hours
    that change color
    with the season
I hold the fragile fabric
in my fingers
trying to be careful
    but I see snags
        here and there
    caused by the roughness
    of my hands

Still, it is beautiful
where the light
reflects the brightness
    of moments
I look at it
    try to see the pattern
but I don't have time to count
    the threads

DESTINY

    it is the end we fear
        forgetting
            then
                it does not matter
now is what we have
    we all share this
        destiny

we have this short time
        in between
to become, to be
to love
to decide
        who will remember
        who will mourn

THERESA AND I

we are determined
        Theresa and I
not to be like our mothers
        birthing does not
        sanctify

we bury secrets in the desert
scrub our wounds
        with coarse sand
and leave that arid place
        create ourselves anew
not out of   whole cloth
               as the saying goes
but   bathing our wounds
        with the soothing balm
        of love
desert flowers transplanted
        bloom
            as we can testify

we do not pick at scars
to open ancient injuries
        serves no purpose
yet   history attends us well
        our children will not suffer
            our children
            are born whole

THROUGH THE LOOKING GLASS

so entranced are we
with our own image in the mirror
we do not notice
that like Alice
>we have stepped through
>the looking glass

>>'Twas brillig, and the slithy toves
>>>Did gyre and gimble in the wabe;'

contrariwise
we run to stay in place
believing the tenants
>of Tweedledum and Tweedledee

we stand upside down
pretending to understand
>Jabberwocky

the effect of living backward
makes us giddy
as we hurry away
>from where we want to be

>>'All mimsy were the borogoves
>>>And the mome raths outgrabe'

>>'The time has come,' the Walrus said,
>>>'To talk of many things:'

is the mirror image the right way which
>inside the looking glass

or do we need to turn around
and read the message upside down?

>>'Of shoes — and ships — and sealing wax —
>>>Of cabbages — and kings —'

Alice said, 'It's rather hard to understand . . .
How curiously it twists . . . it is so *very* lonely here . . .
I'm sure I didn't mean . . .'

the mirror has a way of fooling us
with images so real
it's hard to know which way is up
>or what we need to do

>>'And why the sea is boiling hot —
>>>And whether pigs have wings.'

CITY NIGHTS IN WINTER

winter city nights are not soft
no velvet studded sky hanging
stars burnt out in street lights
      daytime warmth
       chilled in concrete
harsh reflections marring
      walls of glass

no forest sounds are here
only broken souls huddled
against the reality
of crumbling cement paths

PRIMEVAL HEART

how fragile the thin veneer
of civilization we pull around us
our savagery cloaked
in designer labels
      we dare not look
      beneath

still   primitive urges surface
        even as we deny
    and violent solutions
        our only considered
          option
    using muscle and might
      instead of mind
        we resist difference
      cannot tolerate ambiguity
      will not compromise

our technology substitutes
    faith and religion
with bellows of
    prehistoric mysticism
under the cloak of civilization
we hide our
    primeval heart

OUR CHILDREN

Our children will inherit what we give them . . .
                        from a Yoruba praise song

The pattern is set
trimmed much too close
to allow for alterations

it could be changed
        by hard work
        and clever patching

if anyone is interested
and dedicated enough
        to do it

SOMETHING LOST

four children die
        from abuse
        every single day
        in the United States
        of America

it is no use blaming God
        or the Devil
we are responsible

somehow we have lost
        something human
the ability to care
        for those less fortunate
the capacity to share
        with those in need

the Devil does not kill
        our young
God does not abuse
        mothers
        and children

we are responsible

RAGE OF POETRY

my pen hemorrhaged
a rage of poetry
        as if its eruption
        could make a difference

leaking
        passionate smudges
        against injustice

and now my pen is dry
        empty
        as am I

NOW THAT IT IS WINTER

I saw him in the spring
        beside a busy street
curled, asleep
        under a small
        struggling tree

a butterfly lit
        on his shoulder
tiny, bright-winged
        messenger
        of hope

I doubt he saw the butterfly
for he did not move
as the butterfly
        opened its wings
                to the sun

now I wonder
        did the butterfly
        leave in the fall
and where does the man
        sleep
        now that it is winter

SOLDIER BOYS

not to know what happened
before one was born
is always to be a child   Cicero

they play their father's games
not knowing the rules
        there are no rules
they follow the leader
the leader is loud
        "I will be king
        of the hill"
they do what Simon says
        they are haunted
        by ghosts

SING ME NO WARRIOR SONGS

history books stand
        row on row
line after line calling attention
        to war
after war   after war

the earth is sodden
        with the blood
        of fallen heroes
killers and the killed interred
where breezes   instead
        should play
        with laughing children

wars are not for winning
        what victory in blood?
no peace has come
        with this sacrifice
these heroes shape no future
and   flowers do not bloom
        in rotting soil

where are the stories
of those who must
        rebuild
        must tell the children
        of fathers never to return
what history books
sing their songs?

1989

we love to live on the edge

ominous tides swell
        crash explosively
        against our shore

on the precipice we are
unmindful
of erosion below
we denounce the torrent's
        undertow

when   finally
everything breaks
        apart
        it is not our fault

WILL WE NEVER LEARN

don't ask young men
eager to prove machismo
        flexing muscles
        posing grand
            in uniform
ask mothers
remembering birth
        feeling the touch of plump fingers
        tugging still
            the empty place of heart
ask history
what we have learned
        page after page
        filled with terror
            and destruction

there must be a better way
(surely civilization progresses)
        when all the flowers are gone
            will we learn?

CAN IT BE A LOVE SONG

can it be a love song
        without words
a romantic play
        without violins
can it be a poem
        if it doesn't rhyme
is it peace
        just because it isn't war

what about all the children
        who are hungry
and all the people
        who have no home

A BRIGHT RED TULIP

Spring decries
the foolishness of war
        with riotous colors
dandelions dance on the green
flowering trees sway in the breeze
butterflies flutter
birds mock with sweet songs
        the angry sounds
        of snipers

In the rubble
a bright red tulip
    shines
    glorious
        unnoticed
the blood red of violence
    overwhelms

Seasons come and go
    wiser than war
    and warriors
reclaiming ruins
    with moss and vines
        and bright red tulips

NAMING REALITY

"American Nuclear Guinea Pigs: Three Decades of Radiation Experiments on U.S. Citizens" — mid 1980 Congressional report for the victims of Government radiation tests

who can name reality
tell, with certainty, the past
      already tomorrow
      is yesterday
my bones glow into infinity

dark secrets hidden away
      scurry
from the light of day
      where father
does not know my name
or care if i suffer
      unmentionable pain

FALL 1992

        changing now to gold
the honey locust
casts a colorful shadow
      across our garden wall

it seems peaceful
      in this autumn place
      filled with the happy rustle
          of dry leaves underfoot
      and south-bound bird calls
        overhead

but war is here
      though undeclared
anger, hate and fear
change this technicolor time
to drab, stark
          black and white

THE STONE OF REMEMBRANCE
(history)

The past is hidden in darkness
we cannot see
        the future trail
                ancient markings
                carved in stone
                are hidden from our eyes

We scorn the tools left for our hands
cannot accept
        the teachings drawn
        in wondrous colors
                along the path
                we refuse to see

We struggle unlearned
incapable of rolling over
        the stone incised
        with secrets of survival
        blindly stepping off the path
        plowed for us
                we chain ourselves
                to the very stone
                we refuse to see
we are prisoners of history

IT SHOULDN'T HAVE BEEN LIKE THAT

childhood should have been
        a time for learning
        a time to make mistakes
                safely
        a time to stretch muscle and mind
                to learn worth and ability

a time to dream dreams

it shouldn't
        have been spent lonely and afraid
        hungry for something
                unrealized
        bruised and angry
                hurt numbed by drugs
                fear turned into rage
        unable to dream

        dead at seventeen

it shouldn't have been like that

WHERE CHILDREN PLAY

there should be laughter
    where children play
there should be soft grass
and birds singing

there should not be eyes too wise
    burning life away
nor hunger pangs
and anger raging

where children play
there should be
    laughter ringing

BLOOD BROTHERS

divided by miles
    or mountains or seas
young boys
    running, tumbling
        on grass
        or asphalt
    exuberant youth
        everywhere
joining friends with
    pin pricked fingers
    touching in ritual
        blood brothers

too soon
    yearning
    manly powers
donning uniforms
strutting weapons in hand
now
    strangers meet
        bullets
        tear at life
youth draining into puddles
that run the street
    and mix
    together
blood brothers

SAME OL' SNAKE
(Racism — 1990)

that ol' snake is still here
wearin' a new skin
hopin' we won't recognize it

        slitherin' around
        hissin' and rattlin'
        spreadin' poison
        killin' us for
                pure wickedness

that same ol' snake

DEJA VU

    acrid odors rise
            smoke
    vapor fingers
    curl upward
    obliterating
           moon and stars

    wood rough-turned
            cross
    done up in coarse
    woven cloth
    torch flames crack
            night silence

    coward shadows
            creep
    coals burn feverish
    singe edges of security
    fire tongues lick
            white conscience
            shriveling
            icy hearts

NO MORE NEW LAND

Life is here
>or nowhere
there is no escape

every part of this orb
>is recorded
>from the moon

This air — water — earth
this is our place of life
>there are no more
>new lands

THE GARDEN

we have not gone far
>from the garden
we carry its soil beneath
>our nails
and blood flows free
>from scratches and tears
>where thorns and brambles
>caught at us as we left

our need is still for the garden
we long to plunge our hands in mud
>to wrap our wounds in leaves
and eat the bitter fruit hanging

the garden holds
>our ancient secrets
we dare not remember
>our past
violence reminds
>with scars and deep desire
>what primitive urges
>still infect us   hold us fast
>>tie us to the garden
>>we try to leave

LAND OF MY YOUTH

The land of my youth
                is no more.
gone   are clear skies
        and sparkling streams.

Now the air is foul,
              dimming my eyes
the water spoiled,
              leaving me thirsty,
and rocks
torn from the earth
              radiate destruction
causing me   to wither
my parched skin
              stretching over
              dry bones.

WHY ARE WE HERE?

I am not mother
        nor have one
                nor father
the land is putrid
with the stink
        of shallow
                graves
ghosts obscure
        the light

I have filled my lamp
        with oil
trimmed the wick
        with care
I could tell you
        what I know
my bones are long
and in the dark
        they glow

history echoes
        excruciating pain
that plugged ears
        cannot hear
but I am not mother
and the question
        still remains

ONCE I FLEW

once I flew above
    luminous
      churning clouds
and looked down
    on seas and lands
        foreign
        and wonderful

in quiet villages
I listened to words
    alien to me
tasted strange
    spiced food
in bustling bazaars
filled with marvelous things

now I find new adventures
    await me here
treasures of familiarity
I had once been
    too far away
        to see

NOT A PEARL

i would not be a pearl
    insulated in beauty
or a diamond
    hard and cold

perhaps
a drop of water
    to travel in a cloud
    swim a mighty river
    or explore the ocean deep

i'd help to make a rainbow
    for dreamers
a snowflake
    dancing winter
a shower
    heralding spring
i'd be renewed forever
    and always find a welcome
    in some thirsty land

MEMORIES GO

Memories go —
        thankfully
and come back again
        mercifully veiled
flirt —   hopefully
tease —   painfully

and come back again —
            always

I AM THERE
(Zimbabwe)

        Sometimes,
Teasing my ear,
    I hear
The slap of sandaled feet
On red clay-packed paths.
        And I think I am there.

Or I feel warm circles
        Of sun
Filtering green
Through jacaranda leaves,
Warming my skin,
Making me think
        I am there.

        Sometimes
I see bright flashes
Of red-orange, purple
And yellow flowers
Dancing in the treetops.
Scenting the breeze
Cooling my skin
And making me feel
        I am there.

Or I hear the soft voice
        Of Matilda
Between the raindrops
And over the wind,
Waking me
Lonesome,
        Calling me there.

A TIME WHEN ZIMBABWE WAS RHODESIA

the missionary couple (European)
talked of their servant (African)
    in front of him
as if he were invisible or deaf
    or ignorant
and called him "boy"

    but he was none of these
a man, well-educated, traveled
choosing a servant's life to be
    near his children
working on the mission for people
who made no effort to know him
    and called him "boy"

and the missionary thought him
    ignorant

APARTHEID

Passions
    hang heavy
flashing and cracking
    they sear the earth

Passions
    caught up
    as in a whirl-wind
flailing and thrashing
    they beat upon the earth

The earth cannot bear such passion

Children hauled in truck-loads
    to prison
Families weep
tears mingle with the blood
    of the slain

Apartheid   hate
                hate

The earth cannot bear
    such passion

ELDER SISTER

she is my elder sister
    ebony-dark
        and strong
how else could she survive
    uneducated
she works the fields
carries water
    on her head
    and firewood
        gently cradles babies
her sinewy hands
    coax curls into neat plaits
    and tough grass into baskets
        of great beauty
she suffers indignity
    with grace
poverty
    with cleverness
fear and tragedy
    with humor and wisdom
my ebony-dark
    elder sister

SOWETO SCHOOL GIRL

"we who live must do a harder thing than dying is. For
we must think — and ghosts shall drive us on."
                            Howard Thurman, 1965

A bullet chose her
a police bullet
    in a school yard
        in South Africa

One day a playful child
    a singer of songs
    (hoping she will be pretty
        when she is grown)
One day —
    the same day
a corpse
    not singing
    not pretty   at all
    hopes smashed
    dreams gone
        — a ghost
chosen by a bullet

THE ACACIA TREE

The Acacia tree spreads
      branches wide
        under the bright African sun
casting intricate, patterned shadows
on soil smoothed by barefooted children
        who wore its flowers in their hair

      ancestors of children
           far away
      walking a strange land
      never knowing Acacia's smell

      they belong now to another
      place   (their tears have made it
      so)   they cannot remember
      the Acacia
      the warm soil beneath its limbs
          the songs they sing
      now carry only murmurs
          of the past

the Acacia knows none of this —
sending its roots deep into the soil
to entwine with bones
that once danced, fleshed
          in its shadow —
spreading its branches in the sun

SOMETIMES I DREAM YOU
for Grace and Ronald

sometimes
I dream you back to Como Avenue
      or Perry Place
under banana tree and
      tangerine
to share roasted meat, pumpkin leaves
      itshwala and beans
knitting ties that stretch
      half-way round the world
and do not break with years

BONDS OF FAMILY
for Godfrey and Catherine

at once strange and familiar
        Zimbabwe claimed us
bonds forged at Dadaya
        are stronger than blood

reaching from there to here
we weave
        bonds of love
        into family

AFRICAN RIVER

        in season
the rains come
        crashing
        and splashing
carving a frantic course
down rocky slopes
        transforming
and greening the land
as it gathers force

        deepening in pools
that slow the rush
fill and overflow
        become a river
widening and spilling
    .   over rocks
        smooth as glass

playfully gathering from its banks
        small darkly gleaming
        naked boys
tumbling them to the pool below
        mixing laughter
        with frothy spray
flung in droplets
        that reflect
fleeting rainbows
in the brilliant sun

on its way
        serious now
the river slowly spreads
across the valley
bringing succor to the
        thirsty land

DAUGHTERS OF EVE

(. . . a single female . . . in Africa is an ancestor of everyone on earth today.) TIME, 1/26/87

there burned in Eve a desire
    to understand—
        herself   humanity

forced from the garden she struggled on her own
until   at last frustrated
    she reached inside and
        tore her soul to shreds
then flung the bits and pieces across the blackened sky
where they burned brighter than the stars
and showered down upon
    the earth

young girls everywhere gathered the precious embers
and pressed them into the hearts
    of their daughters

we are "old souls" out of time and place
    daughters
    remnants of Eve
carrying in our hearts the unquenchable desire
    to know.

WE ARE ALL GOD'S CHILDREN

eve's blood still flows
    we are brothers and sisters
in our veins the seed unites us
    "yet we do not know each other"
blood ties us together
    we are related
our hearts pumping a primal rhythm
    "still we do not know each other"
it is too hard to carry each other's sorrow
too hard to share good fortune
we are brothers and sisters
    tied together by blood
(we do not know each other at all)

we are all God's children

STORM WARNING

the night is dark
bereft of stars
    and moon
thunder clouds
roil the horizon
rumble lightning
    patterns
    on my wall
electric night
interrupts my lonely
    dream
and I wonder
in my sleeplessness
    what sky
    is over you

VIEW OUT OF AFRICA
26 June 1993

your call came from Africa
echoing memories past
I know you are reality
    feasting with friends
while I am imagination
    relying on photographs
    and fantasy

and on this day, above your call
    astronauts relay
"the view out of Africa is beautiful"
    such is their perspective
reality and fantasy joined
    a technological vision
    without pain
        or friends
a print on glass
    reflecting
    the view out of Africa

THEY TAP AT MY WINDOW

they tap at my window
        starving with bloated bellies
        hurt with wounds gaping
big-eyed children tap
        and tap — and tap
my heart breaks —
        how can my window stay intact

CHINESE SISTER
for Yun (June 1989)

The seeds of democracy
were sown
        in Tiananmen Square
Buds too-soon bloomed
nourished by the blood
        of students
                uncounted
who gave their lives
        bravely

Now roots have spread
beneath the paving stones
        of Tiananmen Square
Rhizomes sprout
        everywhere
        unseen in the vastness
        of the country
protected by parents
        whose children died
                for freedom

Sister, how will those old men
re-write you
        as they seek
                to change
                      history
Must you join
those unseen, unknown
of the world
        who dare not speak
        who can only dream
                of freedom?

FOREVER ON THE WING

there is no passion
    in hopelessness
like too much order
      kills the beauty
      of art

imagination should fly
      with hope
soar
      forever on the wing

IN THE STILLNESS

stillness is the place
where poetry and beauty lie
a time alone with self
    and truth

the small time of quiet
      before night gives way
          to light
          and bird songs

in the still moment
we most clearly see
      our own vision
        of life
        and death

the moment when
      the frightening power
of the mind holds sway
before the thundering
    of the day
    begins
the time when a poem
    or song
        is born

THE POET

the poet lives at the bend
            of moonlight
bright ripples flow from there
            like a river
carrying the poet's music
                        mysterious harmonies
to the place
where I stand waiting

            in my room
moonlight paints the poet's
rhythms in leaf patterns
                        strange images
on the paper shade
over my window
            poem shadows
            from the bend
            of moonlight
                        through my tree

RED BRICK HOUSE

along the river there is a red brick house
with window frames of blue and yellow
and a wonderful wooden porch painted
            purple and green and blue

maybe the local hardware store
offered a sale on small cans
            of rainbow colored paint
or perhaps a poet lives in that red brick house
a poet who sits on the porch in the evening
listening to the wind high in the trees
            and watching barges on the river
                        come and go

I'll never know of course
            we live so far away
but I like to think a poet lives
in the red brick house
            a poet who sits
            on the colorful porch
            and watches the river flow

BORN OF EARTH AND SUN

a poem —
born of earth
    and sun
             — like fruit
blooms flowering boughs
dances on wind
      fragrant in the warm
      spring night
petals sweet
      like the ache of love

a luscious poem —
juicy and pungent
              — like fruit
drops colorful blossoms
    on lush new grass
spilling delectable ripe seeds
    on fertile soil
      where new growth
fulfills a craving
    for truth

THE NATURE OF MY SOUL

on my slow walk home
it is the common ordinary things
that overflow my soul

the bright blue flower thrusting
      its spike through winter's decay
        to herald spring

the birds that chirp to welcome dawn
the fat ducks waddling across our lawn

the apple tree beside our door
    its fruiting
    ripens fall
and winter trees whose wet black branches
    lace against the sky

I need to share this walk with you
to fulfil my spirit's yearning
and bare
before our destination's reached
    the nature
    of my soul

WALKING IN OBSCURITY

I like walking
        in obscurity
my footprints blown
        as dust in wind
my name forgotten
        as the dust

it is the walk that matters
        not notoriety

THE SKIPPING STONE
(for Thoko and Antonio)

the lake
        holding bits
        of summer sun
lapped greedily at the shore
sucking sand from beneath
our feet
        giggling
we searched the shallows
for the perfect stone
        to skip
        across the waves
I can still see you
        poised
        a silhouette
against the sparkling water
then skillfully
        skipping
        your stone
              three times
how many summers will it take
for the sifting sand
        and moving water
to bring that stone
        to shore again
for some other child
to find   and skip

BAREFOOT IN SUMMER

sometimes —
living is like
    being
a barefoot child
        in summer
we hop and limp
over stones
    hot asphalt
    and thorn patches
ever thankful
    for grassy spots
    dappled shade
and the rare cool gift
        of a shower
    from a neighbor's
    lawn sprinkler

SUMMER SOLSTICE

i become lethargic
    these damp
    dark
    cloudy days
filled with a lassitude
    that steals
    energy
    and imagination
this too-wet spring is full of rot
i long for season's turning
    bright blue skies
    the falling colors
    of leaves
frost wrapped nights
    that invigorate
    and crisp
    the days
the intoxicant of summer
    disappoints
i would be filled of autumn
    colors
    to last
    winter's cold

THROUGH YUN'S EYES

my familiar
seen through Yun's eyes
becomes
        wondrous

I keep her collection of stones
in a basket near my door
each one a marvel
        to see, to feel

on my window sill
the dried seed puff
she picked
        still tightly clings
        to stem
silver, feathery beauty
among the green

the small birds rustling
among dried leaves
becomes a song
        heralding winter
a winter that will
sparkle, crystal clear
        seen though Yun's eyes

I LIKE TO FEEL YOU NEAR

I like to feel you near
        to know you will
        come to the doorway
        and read me a poem

I want to lean
        my head on your chest
        when I am tired
        or discouraged

I listen for your footstep
        (quiet not to wake me)
        as you prepare to leave
        for work

I do not want to miss
        any of the time
        we can be near

UNFOCUSED

i am unfocused
like an absentminded rain
that falls randomly
not doing much in any one place
but adding to the flood
      all the same

GOOD THINGS

do I really need

    a refrigerator
    that spits ice cubes
    through its door

    a fax machine
    to send me messages
    I do not want

    a two screen TV
    to show me two programs
    I do not like

    a talking car
    to let me know
    the door is open

    electric kitchen gadgets
    for chores
    I don't do

I don't even like ice cubes

NIGHTMARE

    thoughts suspended in the night
    hang heavy globs
        memories
          or grief congealed
    until the kindly light of moon
    washes over all
        calmly flooding anxiety
    to vapor disappears
    leaving sleep disturbed
        with unremembered
        fears

CANYON WALK

Let us turn from the leaving-road
to walk the canyon floor — one last time
listen just once more to the river —
rushing somewhere over rocks

watch the sun, slowly, color canyon walls warm
feel the chill of sudden shade
where damp has trickled from the top
to mark on rock a pattern weavers envy

listen to the crunch of leaves
adorning red and gold our trail
see the mule deer — wary-eared
breakfast in the tall dry grass

remember how the moon spilled its silver
down cliff walls shining trees and grass
and finally flowing with the river
into the early morning canyon

how long purple shadows caught us up at dusk
hiding trails and trees in the quiet dark
enhancing river songs
and glowing stars above

now walking hand in hand
we are content
        canyon dreams fulfilled
replete with beauty
      — and love

MY TREASURE

It is the small moments
    I treasure
the ones that slip
    through time
    like quicksilver
adding a comforting sheen
    to memories

    memories like
walking with you
    talking
holding hands
    and talking
your arms around me
    passion spent
        talking

CALL OF THE CANYON

I am called to the canyon
and in its depths I feel
    secure.
The river sings its ancient song
rushing over stones
and carving its way
    deeper and deeper
    into the earth.
Above me the canyon walls —
    marked in swirls,
    carved by water,
    swept by winds —
reveal the past
    in layers
    of gold and red.
Now I am part
    of history.
At last,
    I walk on the soil
    of my ancestors.
I move with the rhythm
    of the ages
    into the cradle
    of the earth.

AFTERWORD
by Leon Knight

Ginny Knight created herself.

Her birth certificate reads "Virginia Grant" — Grant after her father who abandoned the family when she was a toddler, and Virginia because her childlike and incompetent mother happened to be born in West Virginia.

Whatever she knows about her family, she learned in bits and pieces as an adult — that she has an older half-sister; that her grandfather, whom she never saw, was alive until she was eight-years-old; that she had a great-grandmother who was an American Indian from the plains of Kansas; that 13-generations ago the original Grant was brought to New England (from Scotland) as an indentured servant after being captured as a prisoner-of-war.

Aside from her great-aunt who raised her until her death when Ginny was ten, the only "relative" Ginny knew was Lucy. In another "family secret" that was not revealed until years after Lucy's death, Lucy was Ginny's aunt — the illegitimate daughter of Ginny's maternal grandfather.

But even with her original family being so dysfunctional, Ginny has not only survived but thrived as a creative person — accomplished artist, award-winning designer and moving poet — and as a generous-hearted, loving person. The grandmother in a mixed-race family, she now not only has extended "family" here in America but "sisters" around the world — especially Matilda Kapala in Zimbabwe, Grace Sibanda in Botswana and Zhang Yun in China.

After growing up feeling unloved and disconnected, Ginny knows and treasures loving connections, wherever they may be found. And these connections have especially been found with her grandchildren Thoko and Antonio and with her niece Theresa.

Thus, although she started life as " . . . a stranger. I have no history" and has lived with leukemia since 1978, she can now claim that "I feel secure" because "I walk on the soil of my ancestors."

As her mate since 1956, I hope that I have contributed to "the small moments" that have, over the years, added "a comforting sheen to memories."